THE *CRYPTOGIC*™ PASSWORD PROTOCOL

Sean Gilbertson
Murli Bhamidipati

ATHENA PRESS
LONDON

THE *CRYPTOGIC*™ PASSWORD PROTOCOL
Copyright © Sean Gilbertson & Murli Bhamidipati 2004

ISBN 1 84401 251 4

First Published 2004 by
ATHENA PRESS
Queen's House, 2 Holly Road
Twickenham TW1 4EG
United Kingdom

Printed for Athena Press

THE *CRYPTOGIC*™
PASSWORD PROTOCOL

Contents

1. Fast Track to *Cryptogic*™

We strongly recommend that you read the whole of this document carefully. However, if you have only a few minutes, you might want to try going straight to the examples in section 7.

2. The Password Problem

Passwords remain a big headache in modern computing. Because of their differing aims, users and designers of computer systems tug in opposite directions:

- System users want simple, easy to remember passwords that grant easy access.

- System designers want unique, hard-to-guess and complex passwords for each system. Then, to add insult to injury, they insist that passwords may not be written down or recorded.

Faced with the conflicting objectives of the designers, most computer users either:

- Use easy-to-guess passwords;

- Use the same password across all systems;

- Keep written records of their passwords;

- Simply forget passwords from time to time; or

- Suffer through a combination of the above approaches!

Passwords constitute the final decision in either granting or denying access to trading systems, online banking or payment systems, ordering systems, corporate networks and confidential documents. Despite all the sophisticated data encryption systems available today, passwords typically remain the weakest link in the security chain. No matter how complex a system's security, the correct password still grants access! So, it's worth having a robust password system.

The *Cryptogic*™ Password Protocol has been developed specifically to address these issues and delivers the following:

a. *Cryptogic*™ users have different and sophisticated passwords for different websites or applications;

b. No written or electronic records of *Cryptogic*™ passwords need exist;

c. There is no limit to the number of passwords which can be managed by the *Cryptogic*™ Password Protocol; and

d. Having mastered the very simple *Cryptogic*™ technique, there is no need to memorise passwords and as a result passwords are rarely forgotten.

3. Getting Started (and Step A: The Fixed Part)

Cryptogic™ passwords are always made up of two parts: a Fixed Part and a Variable Part. There are three simple steps to using *Cryptogic*™:

A. Decide on a FIXED PART. The Fixed Part never changes and is typically made up of words or letters.

B. Decide on a SINGLE RULE which you will use to derive the VARIABLE PART from the system you're logging into. The Variable Part typically produces numbers.

C. Decide HOW TO ADD the Variable Part to the Fixed Part.

IMPORTANT: Having done this, you should *never* reveal anything about your Fixed Part or Variable Part to anyone!

As its name suggests, the Fixed Part remains the same across all passwords. The Fixed Part is entirely up to you and is typically made up of alphabetical letters. So, simply choose the words or letters you want!

.Tips on choosing your Fixed Part:

- Examples of simple Fixed Parts: redcars, lovedancing, everyYEAR (this last example mixes upper and lower case letters for even better security).

- Examples of complex Fixed Parts: RsQNrXt, Kj390rsF, six?!4$3IR.

NOTE: As thousands of people read this document, please don't use any of the sample Fixed Parts shown here – use your own!

- While your Fixed Part can also contain numbers if you want it to, your Variable Part (see later) will produce numbers to be added to your Fixed Part. Accordingly, it is not strictly necessary to include numbers in your Fixed Part although doing so will make your Fixed Part more secure.

- Because it stays the same across all passwords and is accordingly easy to remember, it's worth making your Fixed Part fairly complex.

- UPPER and lower cases: most websites distinguish between upper and lower case and using a combination of cases will make your Fixed Part more secure.

- Including symbols or characters (e.g. '%', '&', '?', etc.): symbols or characters can make your Fixed Part more secure although some websites prohibit the use of special characters. On the whole, we'd suggest you exclude special characters from your Fixed Part.

- While it's much safer to do so using *Cryptogic*™, you should still steer clear of using obvious things such as your initials, date of birth, etc. in your Fixed Part.

- Generally, the longer the Fixed Part, the more secure things are. However, it's quite common for websites to place length restrictions on passwords. Also bear in mind that your Variable Part will add further length to your password. As a rule of thumb, a Fixed Part of 5 to 10 characters should serve you well.

For illustrative purposes only, assume that you choose the following Fixed Part (which, for the remainder of this document, will always be shown in *italics*):

fixed

Having determined your Fixed Part (which never changes unless you want it to), you now need to decide on a process for deriving your Variable Part.

4. Step B: The Variable Part

The Variable Part is always determined by applying a rule of your choice to the system you are logging into. So, if you're logging into a website, you would apply your rule to the name of the website to derive your Variable Part. If you are logging into a network, you would apply your rule to the name of the network. For protected files, you would simply apply your rule to the file's name.

All you need to decide is what rule to use. Once you've chosen your rule, your Variable Part is always based on the same process.

Let's look at a very simple example. Assume your rule is that your Variable Part is simply the number of characters in the name of the website (or file or system) that you're logging into. So, if you were logging into eBay, your Variable Part would be '4' (because there are 4 letters in 'eBay'). If you were logging into Amazon, your Variable Part would be '6', and so on.

There are many ways in which you can derive your Variable Part (ranging from simple through complex) and further examples are given in section 6.

5. Step C: Combining the Fixed and Variable Parts

The simplest way to combine your Fixed and Variable Parts is to add the Variable Part to the end of the Fixed Part. In our example, we previously chose the word 'fixed' as the Fixed Part and decided that the Variable Part would simply be the number of characters in the name of whatever we are logging into. So, if we are logging into eBay, the complete password would be:

*fixed*4

Using the same process, the password for Amazon would be:

*fixed*6

As a third example, if you are logging into Travelocity, the password would be:

*fixed*11

And similarly, if you were logging into a file called 'clientlist', the password would be:

*fixed*10

As you can see, we've created a very simple process that produces a different password for different websites (and files) without the need to remember each password individually!

In this way, and even if you have thousands of passwords, you only need to remember three things which always stay the same:

A. Your Fixed Part (i.e. '*fixed*' in the example above);

B. Your rule for deriving your Variable Part from what you're logging into (i.e. in the example above, the number of characters in the name of what you're logging into); and

C. How to add the Variable Part to the Fixed Part to make up the final password (i.e. in the example above, add the number of characters to the end of the Fixed Part).

Note that the above example is intentionally simple and would produce the same password for any two websites (or files or systems) which have the same number of characters in their names. So, let's look at more sophisticated solutions in the next two sections.

6. More on Step B: Better Variable Parts

In our previous simple example, we decided to derive the Variable Part by simply counting the number of characters in the name of whatever we're logging into.

There are many other rules you can use to determine the Variable Part from the name of whatever you're logging into. For example:

a) Count the number of vowels (i.e. the letters 'a', 'e', 'i', 'o', 'u') in the name of whatever you're logging into. So, for 'Yahoo' you would get '3' and for 'eBay' you would get '2'.

b) Count the number of consonants (i.e. any letters except 'a', 'e', 'i', 'o', 'u') in the name of whatever you're logging into. So, for 'Yahoo' you would get '2' and for 'Amazon' you would get '3'.

c) Count the number of syllables in the name of whatever you're logging into. So, for 'Yahoo' you would get '2' ('Ya' and 'hoo') and for 'Amazon' you would get '3' ('A', 'ma' and 'zon').

d) Assign a number to each letter in the alphabet: a=1, b=2, c=3, etc as follows:

a	b	c	d	e	f	g	h	i	j	k	l	m
1	2	3	4	5	6	7	8	9	10	11	12	13

n	o	p	q	r	s	t	u	v	w	x	y	z
14	15	16	17	18	19	20	21	22	23	24	25	26

Using this technique, you can 'translate' each letter in the name of the website (or network or file) into a number. So, if you were logging into eBay, your Variable Part would be 52125 (because e=5, B=2, a=1, y=25). Your completed password would then be:

*fixed*52125

Rather than translating *all* the letters in the name, you could of course decide to use only the first two letters, or the first and last, or any other selection you like.

For an interesting twist on this technique, you could reverse the alphabet in the above table such that a=26, b=25, c=24, etc.

e) Count the number of times a particular letter (or combination of letters of your choice) appears in the name of what you're logging into. So, if your first name is Mary and you're logging into eBay, your Variable Part would be 2 (as 'a' and 'y' appear in 'eBay' and in 'Mary'). If however your name is John, your Variable Part when logging into eBay would be 0. Similarly, if you choose to count the number of times the letter 'a' (for example) appears in the name of what you're logging into, you would get 1 for 'eBay' and 2 for 'Amazon'.

f) In the examples thus far, the Variable Part has always produced numbers from whatever you are logging into. It is of course also possible to take letters from whatever you're logging into. So, for example, you could decide simply to add to your Fixed Part the last two letters (say, capitalised) of what you're logging into. So, your Variable Part for Amazon would be 'ON' and your complete password would be:

*fixed*ON

For eBay, your Variable Part would be 'AY' and your complete password would be:

*fixed*AY

As was the case with numbers, there are several twists which can be employed in deriving letters for the Variable Part. Let's look at one example.

Rather than using the letters exactly as they appear in the name of whatever you're logging into, you could 'shift' to the letter which appears two positions to the right in the alphabet (i.e. a=c, b=d, c=e, etc). So, in effect, you would 'translate' any letter appearing in the name of whatever you're logging into using the following table:

a	b	c	d	e	f	g	h	i	j	k	l	m
c	d	e	f	g	h	i	j	k	l	m	n	o

n	o	p	q	r	s	t	u	v	w	x	y	z
p	q	r	s	t	u	v	w	x	y	z	a	b

So, the password for logging into Amazon would be:

*fixed*QP

because 'O' becomes 'Q' and 'N' becomes 'P'.

g) In our examples so far, we have always added the Variable Part to the end of the Fixed Part. Positioning the Variable Part with respect to the Fixed Part can take many forms and, for example, you could:

- Place the Variable Part before the Fixed Part.

- Place a portion of your Variable Part before and another portion after the Fixed Part.

- Insert part or all of the Variable Part in the middle of the Fixed Part or at some other fixed position.

- Get fairly complex and let the position of your Variable Part inside the Fixed Part be determined by what you're logging into (for example, the number of vowels). So, if your Variable Part is determined by the number of letters in the name of what you're logging into, and the position of the Variable Part is determined by the number of vowels in what you're logging into, your completed password for logging into Amazon would be:

fix6ed

- (because there are 6 letters in 'Amazon' and 3 vowels ('a', 'a' and 'o') so the '6' should be place after the 3rd letter of the Fixed Part). The same approach applied to eBay would produce the following completed password:

fi4xed

- (because there are 4 letters in 'eBay' and 2 vowels ('e' and 'a') so the '4' is placed after the 2nd letter in the Fixed Part).

h) Lastly, and rather than using only one of the above examples for deriving the Variable Part, you might want to consider using more than one approach simultaneously. So, let's say you decide that your Variable Part will comprise:

- The first two letters (converted to capital letters) of what you're logging into (to be placed before the Fixed Part); and

- The number of vowels (a, e, i, o, u) in the name of what you're logging into (to be placed at the end of the Fixed Part).

Using this approach for logging into Amazon would produce the following completed password:

AM*fixed*3

Logging into eBay using the same approach would produce the following completed password:

EB*fixed*2

The methods described above are by no means the only way of deriving Variable Parts so feel free to invent your own!

7. Summary and Examples

In summary then, the *Cryptogic*™ Password Protocol has three simple steps:

A. Decide on any Fixed Part you like comprising any combination of letters – it will remain the same in all your passwords across all applications;

B. Choose a rule for how to derive your Variable Part from the name of what you're logging into (be it a website name, a file name, a system name, etc.); and

C. Choose a rule for how to combine your Variable Part and your Fixed Part. Again, this rule will remain the same in all your passwords across all applications.

The following examples combine steps B and C and then demonstrate how each arrangement would work for logging into Amazon, eBay and Travelocity.

EXAMPLE 1

Step A: Fixed Part	*fixed* (i.e. any combination of letters you like which will remain the same in all passwords)
Steps B&C: Variable Part	a) Insert the number of letters (in the name of what you're logging into) before the Fixed Part.
	b) Add the first and last letters (in the name of what you're logging into) to the beginning of the sequence obtained from a) above.
Password for 'Amazon':	an6*fixed*
	a) There are 6 letters in 'Amazon'
	b) The first and last letters in 'Amazon' are 'a' and 'n'.
Password for 'eBay':	ey4*fixed*
	a) There are 4 letters in 'eBay'
	b) The first and last letters in 'eBay' are 'e' and 'y'.
Password for 'Travelocity':	ty11*fixed*
	a) There are 11 letters in 'Travelocity'
	b) The first and last letters of 'Travelocity' are 't' and 'y'.

EXAMPLE 2

Step A: Fixed Part	*fixed*
Steps B&C: Variable Part	a) Insert the number of consonants (in the name of what you're logging into) before the Fixed Part. b) Add the number of vowels (in the name of what you're logging into) to the end of the Fixed Part.
Password for 'Amazon':	3*fixed*3 a) There are 3 consonants in 'Amazon' b) There are 3 vowels in 'Amazon'.
Password for 'eBay':	2*fixed*2 a) There are 2 consonants in 'eBay' b) There are 2 vowels in 'eBay'.
Password for 'Travelocity':	7*fixed*4 a) There are 7 consonants in 'Travelocity' b) There are 4 vowels in 'Travelocity'.

EXAMPLE 3

Step A: Fixed Part	*fixed*
Steps B&C: Variable Part	a) Assuming a=1, b=2, c=3, etc, find the position of the first letter (in the name of what you're logging into) in the alphabet and insert this number before the Fixed Part.
	b) Assuming a=1, b=2, c=3, etc, find the position of the last letter (in the name of what you're logging into) in the alphabet and add this number after the Fixed Part.
Password for 'Amazon':	1*fixed*14
	a) The first letter in 'Amazon' is 'a' and 'a' is the first letter of the alphabet.
	b) The last letter in 'Amazon' is 'n' and 'n' is the 14th letter in the alphabet.
Password for 'eBay':	5*fixed*25
	a) The first letter in 'eBay' is 'e' and 'e' is the 5th letter in the alphabet.
	b) The last letter in 'eBay' is 'y' and 'y' is the 25th letter in the alphabet.
Password for 'Travelocity':	20*fixed*25
	a) The first letter in 'Travelocity' is 't' and 't' is the 20th letter in the alphabet.
	b) The last letter in 'Travelocity' is 'y' and 'y' is the 25th letter in the alphabet.

EXAMPLE 4

Step A: Fixed Part	*fixed*
Steps B&C: Variable Part	a) Assume your name is 'Trevor'. Count the number of times the letters in your name appear in the name (of what you're logging into) and insert this number before the Fixed Part.
	b) Count the number of letters (in the name of what you're logging into) and add this number to the end of the Fixed Part.
	c) Take the first two letters (in the name of what you're logging into) and add the first letter to the beginning of the sequence derived from the above steps and the second letter to the end of the sequence.
Password for 'Amazon':	a1*fixed*6n
	a) Only 1 letter ('o') from the name 'Trevor' appears in 'Amazon'.
	b) There are 6 letters in 'Amazon'.
	c) The first letter in 'Amazon' is 'a' and the last is 'n'. These go on either ends of the sequence.
Password for 'eBay':	e1*fixed*4y
	a) Only 1 letter ('e') from the name 'Trevor' appears in 'eBay'.
	b) There are 4 letters in 'eBay'.
	c) The first letter in 'eBay' is 'e' and the last is 'y'. These go on either ends of the sequence.

Password for	t5*fixed*11y
'Travelocity':	a) 5 letters ('t', 'r', 'e', 'v' and 'o') from the name 'Trevor' appear in 'Travelocity'.
	b) There are 11 letters in 'Travelocity'.
	c) The first letter in 'Travelocity' is 't' and the last is 'y'. These go on either ends of the sequence.

The above examples demonstrate that the *Cryptogic*™ Password Protocol can be used to develop almost any number of possible combinations, from very simple to very complex.

Several complex methods can be developed by inserting different portions of the Variable Part at floating positions in the Fixed Part. For example, you could count the number of syllables in the name of whatever you're logging into and, after that many positions in your Fixed Part, insert into the Fixed Part the first letter in the name of whatever you're logging into. As a second floating insertion, you could count the number of times the letters from your first name occur in whatever you're logging into and insert that after the nth letter of the Fixed Part where n is determined by the number of vowels in the name of whatever you're logging into.

Remember: never disclose information about any of your steps to any other person.

8. Limitations of *Cryptogic*™

Cryptogic™ works wherever you have full control over what the password is. *Cryptogic*™ has certain limitations when restrictions are placed on the password by the website, network or system operator.

In the worst case (where you are issued a password which cannot be changed), *Cryptogic*™ cannot work.

Sometimes you are able to determine what the password is but there are special restrictions. For example, passwords may need to be of a particular length, contain special characters or may need to be changed from time to time. *Cryptogic*™ still works in most such instances, although you may need to keep a record of what the restrictions are relating to that particular password. However, note that there is no need to keep a record of the actual password!

Let's look at some of these issues in greater detail in the next two sections.

9. Passwords with Length Restrictions

Some websites force users to have passwords with a minimum and/or maximum number of characters. So, when you apply your personalised *Cryptogic*™ password protocol to that website's name, you might find that it is either too long or too short.

If your *Cryptogic*™ password is too short, it's easiest to start repeating your *Cryptogic*™ password again until you reach the required number of characters. So, if you need a minimum of 10 characters and your *Cryptogic*™ password is '*6fixed3*', simply add enough characters from the beginning of your password to reach 10 characters (i.e. '*6fixed36fi*').

If your *Cryptogic*™ password is too long, it's easiest to remove characters from your *Cryptogic*™ password (either from the front end or the back end, at your discretion) until you reach the required number of characters.

Most websites tell you about length restrictions when you choose your password for the first time. However, when you come back to log in, they rarely remind you of the length restrictions! So, we recommend that you maintain a record of the restrictions imposed by such websites so that you know how to adapt your *Cryptogic*™ password to fit the site. Note that there is no need to record your actual password though!

Cryptogic™ is presently building a database of websites that have such restrictions. Registered *Cryptogic*™ buyers will be able to refer to this database at our website. Feel free to contribute to the database by e-mailing any such restrictions you come across to restricted.site@cryptogic.com

10. Passwords that Require Periodic Changing

Some systems (networks in particular) require that you change your password periodically. After several changes this often becomes annoying, as the system might prevent you from using any previously used password again.

This restriction is best dealt with by keeping a record of how often the password requires changing and when the last change was made.

Cryptogic™ can be adapted to dealing with such restrictions and two examples are discussed below.

- If your password requires changing monthly (or less frequently), you might consider adding the details of the month and year in which you're resetting the password to the end (or beginning or middle) of your regular *Cryptogic*™ password. So, if your regular *Cryptogic*™ password produces '3fix7', you would add something like 'dec03' or 'mar04' to the end of your password to get '3fix7dec03' or '3fix7mar04'. In this way you'll have a unique password every time without the need to remember what you used last.

- If your password requires changing more frequently than monthly, similar logic would apply. However, instead of using the current month as a guide, you could consider adding the week number to the end of your regular *Cryptogic*™ password. So if you are in the 46th week of 2003, you could add '4603' to your regular *Cryptogic*™ password.

Similarly, you could develop a simple code to represent the iteration, period, month or year that you are in. For example, 'A' might represent 1 or January, 'B' could represent 2 or February and so forth. In this way February 2004 would be 'BD' where 'B' represents February and 'D' the '4' in 2004.

11. Applying *Cryptogic*™ to PIN numbers

The *Cryptogic*™ Password Protocol can also be applied to PIN numbers. Because PIN numbers typically contain no letters, you will also need a Fixed Part which contains no letters. The 3 steps however, remain the same:

A. Decide on a Fixed Part you like – it will remain the same in all your PINs. Because most PINs are 4 to 6 digits long, keep your Fixed Part short, say 2-3 characters;

B. Choose a rule for how to derive your Variable Part from the name of the system you're accessing (be it a bank, telephone helpline or alarm system); and

C. Choose a rule for how to add your Variable Part to your Fixed Part.

Because PINs have varying lengths, it is a good idea to keep a record of the length (and only the length!) of the PIN for a given system.

Sometimes the *Cryptogic*™ password system you've selected will produce a PIN which is either too short or too long for a given system. In such cases, simply deploy the extension or shortening mechanisms described in section 9.

An example is shown overleaf:

EXAMPLE 1

Step A: Fixed Part	*73* (stays the same in all PINs)
Steps B&C: Variable Part	a) Count the number of letters (in the name of what you're logging into) and insert this number before the Fixed Part.
	b) Count the number of vowels (in the name of what you're logging into) and insert this number at the end of the Fixed Part.
PIN for 'First Bank' (4 digits required)	9732
	a) There are 9 letters in 'First Bank'.
	b) There are 2 vowels in 'First Bank'.
PIN for 'Office Alarm': (6 digits required)	11735(1)
	a) There are 11 letters in 'Office Alarm'.
	b) There are 5 vowels in 'Office Alarm'.
	c) Because 6 digits are required, simply start repeating the *Cryptogic*™ PIN until the right number of digits is reached (i.e. add the first '1' to the end of the PIN).
PIN for 'Vault' (4 digits required)	5732
	a) There are 5 letters in 'Vault'.
	b) There are 2 vowels in 'Vault'.

12. Conclusion and Feedback

In addition to the benefits we outlined in section 2, *Cryptogic*™ also provides multiple levels of security.

- If someone is able to figure out your Fixed Part, they don't know how to derive your Variable Part.

- Conversely, if they are able to establish how your Variable Part is derived, they still need your Fixed Part. Moreover, they also need to know how to add your Variable Part to the Fixed Part.

- Importantly, and because *Cryptogic*™ generates different passwords for different systems, if security is breached at one site, that password cannot be used to gain access to another system.

We hope you find the *Cryptogic*™ Password Protocol very useful.

As we continually strive to improve the *Cryptogic*™ Password Protocol, your feedback would be greatly appreciated and can be sent to buyer.support@cryptogic.com

The following blank pages are provided for you to experiment with the Cryptogic™ Password Protocol. However, please ensure that they contain no information which could be used by others to obtain any information about your passwords or PIN numbers.

NOTES

NOTES

NOTES

NOTES

NOTES

NOTES

NOTES

NOTES

NOTES

NOTES

NOTES

NOTES

NOTES

NOTES